Original title:
Cactus Chronicles

Copyright © 2025 Creative Arts Management OÜ
All rights reserved.

Author: Nathaniel Blackwood
ISBN HARDBACK: 978-1-80566-597-7
ISBN PAPERBACK: 978-1-80566-882-4

Life Beneath a Thin Skin

In the desert's sunny glare,
I stand with prickles everywhere.
A sun hat wouldn't go amiss,
Too bad I can't hide my spiky bliss.

My friends say I should grow a coat,
But who needs sweaters? I float!
With all this sun, I thrive like mad,
It's the desert life, and I'm quite glad.

Seeking Shade in the Sun

Oh to find a shady nook,
Where I can smile and just cook!
I'll lie beneath a crooked tree,
And raise my arms—come join me!

The sunbeam dance is quite a sight,
But every time, I feel the bite.
With laughter ringing through the air,
I can't deny I love the flair!

The Grace of Green

In a world of sandy brown,
I wave my arms, not wearing frown.
With spindly limbs and tops so bright,
I'm possibly the spikiest sight!

I twirl and sway, oh what a scene,
A dandy bachelor, so evergreen!
While friends may see a pointy face,
I'm a jolly soul in this green place.

Unraveled in the Desert

I tried to wear an outfit cool,
But spikes and sand just are not fuel!
With threads a-flapping, I lost my way,
Now I'm a hazard to those who play.

So here I stand, a sight so grand,
A fashion statement that's not planned.
Among the dunes, I'll strut and cheer,
In my pointy charm, I disappear!

Oasis Reflections

In the desert sun, they strut with pride,
A green parade, where the water's a guide.
They wave their arms in a wacky cheer,
With humor as sharp as their spikes, oh dear!

Sand may roll in, but they sit still,
Laughing at storms with stubborn will.
A mirage of beauty, a comical sight,
Who knew that dry could be this light?

Prickly Dreams

In the land of spikes, the dreams take flight,
Tiny green warriors, ready to bite.
They plot their schemes, it's a funny race,
While dodging the sun, they wear a smiley face.

With friends all around, they dance all night,
Under the stars, such a silly sight.
When morning comes, they yawn with glee,
Who knew being prickly could be so free?

The Resilient Bloom

A flower peeks from a prickly crust,
Glowing with laughter, it's a must.
In a barren land, it throws a party,
Inviting the sun, never too hearty.

With petals so bright, it giggles away,
Challenging drought to ruin the play.
"Bring on the heat!" it shouts with pride,
For within the tough, the joys will abide.

Thorny Tales

Gather 'round folks for tales so sly,
Of prickly heroes that never say die.
They navigate life with a quirk and a twist,
In this spiky world, they do quite persist.

From battles with drought to wind's wild tease,
They laugh in the face of worries with ease.
With thorns for armor, they make their stand,
Jokes like a punchline in this sandy land.

Layers of Solitude

In the desert sun, I stand alone,
My prickly friends, they're on their own.
With layers thick, we keep it cool,
No need for hugs, we play it cool.

They say I'm sharp, but I just smile,
Each needle's point, my little style.
A fortress built of green and pride,
In solitude, I confidently hide.

Brevity of Blooms

A burst of color, then it's gone,
In a blink, my flowers yawn.
What's the rush? Take a seat,
A one-day show, oh what a feat!

My petals flaunt, then fade away,
Just like my social life today.
I try to charm with all my might,
But blooms are brief, oh what a plight!

The Heart of Hardiness

My friends in soil, so tough and rough,
They call me strong, but it's just enough.
With every thorn that I display,
My heart's still soft, or so they say.

Through drought and sun, I hold my ground,
In the desert's heart, I've found my sound.
A hero formed of spines and grit,
With every laugh, I just don't quit!

Spiky Embraces

Come for a hug, but watch your back,
I'm not exactly what you lack.
My love is sharp, my heart's a mess,
A prickly friend, but who would guess?

With tender care, I poke and prod,
A warm embrace? Oh, what a façade!
In spiky love, I find my peace,
A quirky tale that won't quite cease.

Shadows of Succulence

In the sun, they stand so tall,
With prickly spines, they sprawl.
They whisper jokes to the breeze,
While dodging bees with such ease.

A desert dance, a wobbly show,
When the wind begins to blow.
They sway and bend, a sight so funny,
Thinking they're all tough and sunny.

With blooms so bright and colors grand,
They think they're part of a rock band.
But roots are tangled, ouch, oh dear!
What a thorny life, we cheer!

Echoes of the Dunes

In the dunes, they stand and pout,
Wishing for a friendly route.
Each tiny bloom with a bold stance,
Grows like it's ready to dance.

The shadows scratch in playful ways,
Chasing light on sunny days.
With stories etched in grains of sand,
They joke with lizards, hand in hand.

Oh, the sassy tales they weave,
Of desert nights, you won't believe!
They tease the stars in dazzling light,
While giggling all through the night.

Desert's Palette

Colors splash, a lively show,
On prickly greens, oh what a glow!
Like artists with a brush in hand,
Creating wonders across the land.

A yellow flower tries to peek,
Out from shades, feeling quite chic.
While spiky friends gossip nearby,
Rolling their eyes and letting out a sigh.

With hues so bright, they jest and play,
Painting sunsets in their own way.
A prickly laugh, a floral twist,
Who knew the desert could be such a list?

Survival in Solitude

In solitude, they take a stand,
Holding tight to that dry land.
They huddle close, like pals in a row,
Trading secrets that few would know.

With a poke and a jab, they laugh away,
Adapting just to face each day.
Their armor suits hide smiles bright,
Surviving well in day and night.

In the heat, they sing their tune,
Making mirages dance like a cartoon.
For in their thorns, a humor lies,
A prickly jest beneath vast skies.

Sun-Kissed Soliloquy

In the desert, I do sway,
My spines shine bright, come what may.
The sun is hot, I dance with glee,
A prickly ballet, just me and me.

Lizards laugh as I perform,
With every gust, I bend and swarm.
My shadow's small, but spirit grand,
An artist of the barren land.

Fortitude in Flora

Standing tall, I'm full of pride,
Through hardships, I will not hide.
With every poke, a story told,
Of daring dreams and hearts so bold.

A tumbleweed rolls by and grins,
While I make jokes about my sins.
With wit as sharp as my own spikes,
I laugh at life and all its hikes.

Life Interwoven with Spines

In a world of fluff and bloom,
I thrive amidst the dusty gloom.
My friends are thorns, they poke and prod,
Together we form a prickly squad.

Bouncing bunnies skedaddle past,
While I hold laughter, unsurpassed.
"Life's too short," I tell a bee,
"Let's sip some nectar, just us three."

The Poetry of Parched Ground

On this parched and cracked domain,
I sing my songs, both sweet and plain.
   The wind whispers a jolly tune,
   While I sway gently, afternoon.

With each drop of rain, I take a cheer,
   But oh my, the weather's sheer!
   I dream of oceans while I grin,
   In this sandy circus, I find my kin.

Patterns of Persistence

In a desert dance, they stand tall,
Needling the sun with a spiky sprawl.
They thrive in the heat, what a sight!
With laughter in thorns, they spark delight.

Braving the winds with a wobble and sway,
Fashioning hats from the tumbleweed stray.
They humor the lizards, toss back a grin,
Sipping the sunshine—let the fun begin!

Sun-bleached Stories

Once upon a time in the sandy land,
A prickly plant thought it was quite grand.
With stories of how it survived the drought,
Fluffed up its needles, and really knocked out!

It cracked a few jokes with a gecko friend,
While waving its arms like a wild whimsy trend.
Tales of the sun with a sarcastic twist,
Who knew being prickly could be in a list?

Tales from the Parched Earth

In arid lands where the shadows tease,
Prickly pals giggle in the warm breeze.
With each little rain, they dance in delight,
Hoping to sprout a new spiky sight.

They swap their woes over cacti tea,
Ribbing each other till they yell, "Yippee!"
With roots sinking deep, they plot their next feat,
Living their lives on a sunny repeat.

From Dust to Dazzle

From a sprinkle of dust to a dazzling green,
These spiny warriors know how to glean.
With a chuckle and grin, they stand out so bold,
In a world where water is worth its weight in gold.

They laugh at the rain, a rare funny jest,
Prodding their pals, who just want a rest.
Basking in glory, in the sun's warm embrace,
With spirit and humor, they ace the dry race.

Towers of Time

Tall and prickled, reaching up high,
They tickle the clouds as they wave goodbye.
Time seems to stop in their spiky embrace,
While the desert sun draws a smile on each face.

Whispers of history float on the breeze,
As lizards play tag and dance with such ease.
The shadows of towers stretch long and lean,
In this wacky world, nothing's ever routine.

Blossoms in the Barrenness

Amidst dry lands, a splash of bright hue,
Petals in pink like a party for two.
They giggle and chatter, oh what a spree,
In a barren land, they hold a jamboree.

While the sun throws its heat like a warm, fuzzy quilt,
These blooms keep it cool, not a wrinkle or wilt.
With each joyful sway, they tease and they twirl,
In the heart of the dust, they create a grand whirl.

Armor of the Dry

Clad in armor, with spikes all around,
A knight in the desert, so fierce and so proud.
He struts through the sands with a casual flair,
While the critters all cheer, 'Is he really a bear?'

The sun reigns above, but he doesn't mind,
Waving at shadows that dance in the wind.
He's the sultan of prickles, with friends by his side,
In this wild, dry land, there's nowhere to hide!

The Hidden Oasis

In the heart of the cacti, a secret does dwell,
An oasis of laughter where all creatures yell.
With water that sparkles, like diamonds that sing,
It's a splash-tastic party, joy's the main thing.

Palm trees are guests, doing the hula,
While frogs in top hats croon like a true troubadour.
Here in the shade, with no worries or strife,
They toast with coconuts to the joy of life!

Secrets of the Arid Realm

In the land where lizards prance,
The spiky plants hold a playful glance.
Whispers of secrets, they all share,
Of the sun's kiss and a desert's dare.

Prickly parties thrown at dusk,
With drinks of water, sweet and husk.
Sassy needles in a dance,
Making the desert's creatures prance.

Joyful blooms, when night turns bright,
A glimpse of mischief in the twilight.
Who knew such fun lived out here?
In the arid realm, we persevere.

So join the fun, don't be shy,
For life's a laugh 'neath the vast blue sky.
With every poke and prickly grin,
Desert delights will surely win.

Sun-Kissed Stalks

Gather round, the sun is high,
Let's toast to stalks that reach the sky.
They stretch and wiggle, full of cheer,
A sunny dance, let's give a cheer!

With hats of shade, they cool the day,
Making fun of clouds that stray.
They lean, they sway, quite a sight,
Belly laughs under the bright light.

Oh, to be a sun-kissed stalk,
With jokes so funny, they'll make you gawk.
In the heat, the laughs keep coming,
Life in the sun is always humming.

So if you're feeling low and flat,
Join the stalks, just like that.
In their company, you will find,
Joyful giggles that free your mind.

Shadows of the Saguaro

Tall and proud, they cast a shade,
Where cactus creatures like to wade.
Underneath, the critters play,
Finding refuge from the ray.

Saguaro smiles, oh so sly,
Watching shadows dance and fly.
The sun can bake, but we don't mind,
For laughter's easy to find!

With every poke and crooked grin,
They tell you tales of bumpy kin.
Beneath their arms, a comedy show,
Where rows of laughter surely grow.

So let the shadows keep you cool,
In the desert's heart, we all are fools.
Join the fun beneath their sway,
And laugh your worries all away.

Heartbeats in the Sand

In the grains where laughter lands,
We feel the pulse of desert bands.
With tiny critters, oh so spry,
They bop along, don't be shy!

Beneath the stars, the night ignites,
With silliness in our desert sights.
Heartbeat rhythms tap away,
As sand-ducks quack at a bright bouquet.

Wind whispers jokes to the wide expanse,
While scorpions join in a sandy dance.
The heartbeats drum a funny tune,
Beneath the glow of a dreamy moon.

So take a step in this sandy land,
Join the laughter, take my hand.
For here in the dust, with every beat,
Life's a party; isn't it sweet?

Verticals of the Vast

In the desert, the tall ones stand,
Waving arms in a sunburned band.
They dance when the wind gives a shout,
But trip when the visitors stroll about.

The sunblushed green with a prickly smile,
Wonders if it can hug for a while.
But closer you get, then you will know,
Hugs are not free; they come with a foe.

They boast of their height and shadow play,
While critters lounge in their spiky sway.
A bird once tried to nest in a thorn,
Now it claims it's been beaten and worn.

In the vastness of space, they hold the key,
To laughter and joy, though painful, you see.
The parade of the tall, they're hilarious crew,
In a world where advice comes with a view.

Stories Written in Sand and Spine

On golden dunes where tales unfold,
The spine-armed jesters, both brash and bold,
Whisper their secrets through a prickly grin,
As lizards hide from the chaos within.

With each shifting grain, a saga begins,
Of burnt BBQs and invisible wins.
A tumbleweed rolls, making quite a scene,
While the prickly pals mimic a movie screen.

Beach balls bounce past, in the gentle breeze,
They critique the antics with giggles and tease.
Under the sun, they sip on their lore,
As the wind writes a history we can't ignore.

These spiky storytellers, sharp as can be,
Spin tales of the desert, so wild and free.
With laughter and sand, they twirl in delight,
Creating a world, both funny and bright.

Fleeting Fragrance in Harshness

In arid plains where scents seem to hide,
A bloom breaks forth, in cheer and in pride.
It giggles at sunburns, "You can't touch me!"
While perfume wafts by, as sweet as can be.

With petals so bright, it's a wild little act,
A stunt show of color; oh, how it'll attract!
It tickles your nose, not a sting in the air,
But nature's prankster, reminding, "Beware!"

As bees come to tease, they stumble with glee,
Chasing the bloom, as it sways like a spree.
This jester of fragance, it won't last too long,
Yet it fills up the harshness with a spirited song.

In a world where dry is the common refrain,
This lively little flower flips boredom to gain.
Dancing through thorns, what a curious plight,
Fleeting yet funny, it's a pure delight.

A Testament to Tenacity

With roots in the rock and a grin that won't quit,
They whisper, "We thrive; can you handle it?"
A poky parade through the starlit night,
With armor so tough, it's a strange sight.

"Why are we here?" some ask every day,
"To serve up some humor, come what may!"
With each little bloom, they shrug off the doubt,
Showing the world what it's all about.

Through heat waves and storms, they never retreat,
In the desert's wild laughter, they find their beat.
The spines stand tall, while the world shifts and bends,
A charming reminder, that fun never ends.

So here's to their journey, so silly and true,
These spiky comedians, a zany crew.
In a life filled with troubles, they laugh and they shine,
A testament to tenacity, sweet and divine.

Sunscorched Secrets

In the desert's blaze, I lie,
Hats fly off as lizards sigh.
A prickly friend, with arms so wide,
Wonders if I'm a meal that's fried.

The sun's a prankster in disguise,
With flaming rays, it always tries.
Shade is stolen, never given,
Yet laughter dances, skies are riven.

Watched a tumbleweed today,
Thought it might just roll my way.
It danced to beats of unseen bands,
While I searched for some cool strands.

A lizard winks, what a tease,
Wearing shades, undeterred by heat.
I asked if he had any plans,
He just grinned and waved his hands.

Saguaro Memories

In a desert bar, we gather 'round,
With prickly drinks, and laughter sound.
The jukebox plays a twangy tune,
While a sagebrush sings to the moon.

A friend once tried to be a star,
Dressed in green, said he could spar.
With arms like forks, he struck a pose,
But fell headlong among the crows.

Hot wind whispers secrets here,
Of cactus dreams and bottled beer.
Chasing shadows, we slide and dash,
Leaving only a sunburned splash.

The night was young, our spirits high,
We danced under a cactus sky.
In every poke, a tale unspooled,
Of desert nights when we were cool.

Hushed in the Heat

The desert slept, not a sound to hear,
Yet creaky doors kicked up some cheer.
A tumbleweed met a lone, lost shoe,
Declared itself king of the avenue.

In whispers, the succulents plot,
How to cook up a dash in a pot.
With sassy wit, they spice the air,
Mocking tourists without a care.

A rattlesnake served as DJ fine,
With beats that made the cacti shine.
Under the stars, they break and sway,
In this hot life, we shout hooray!

But when the sun comes up to play,
The laughter fades, and shades obey.
The prickly folks just wink, and grin,
Hushed in the heat, let the fun begin.

The April of Arid Lands

April's here, the sun's a tease,
With sandy toes and buzzing bees.
A saguaro sporting flowers bright,
Wonders why it's still a fright.

The sun's a jokester, laughing loud,
Telling tales to the clouded crowd.
"Slip on sandals, it'll be fine,"
While rain clouds say, "Just wait for wine!"

The rabbits hop, with jigs and spins,
Chasing dreams, teasing chins.
While javelinas munch on greens,
They start a dance-off—what a scene!

But oh, the dust storms roll and race,
Yet smiles still bloom, it's quite the chase.
In April heat, the fun expands,
As laughter reclaims these arid lands.

Echoes of the Sandstorm

A tumbleweed rolled by with a grin,
Whispers of mischief begin to spin.
In the desert, the sun has no chill,
But even the lizards know how to thrill.

Dust devils dance with a laugh and a twirl,
Chasing the shadows, giving a whirl.
The cacti wear hats made of sun,
In this sandy circus, we all have fun!

One cactus claimed it could do a backflip,
But all it managed was a small slip.
With arms in the air, it waved with pride,
While the others just snickered, and chuckled wide.

So join in the laughter, don't take it too hard,
Even thorns can make a funny yard.
In this desert, the joy is a blast,
With echoes of giggles that forever last!

Prickly Perspectives

A prickly friend on a sunny day,
In every quirk, there's a funny way.
With arms outstretched like a dance gone wrong,
Our spiky sage sings a bouncy song.

It tells tales of storms and wild nights,
Of tumbleweeds lost in crazy fights.
"Don't take life too serious, just enjoy the view,
Even if it ends with a spiky shoe!"

And so we gather in this oddball crew,
With laughter ringing out, a giggle or two.
A final toast with a saguaro spree,
To the funny looks, as wild as can be!

We poke fun at the grit and the grind,
Finding joy where the sun's unkind.
With humor as bright as the desert expanse,
We celebrate life in a silly dance!

Lushness in the Lean

In a land where the green's just a tease,
A tall, lean fellow sways in the breeze.
With arms that reach but don't quite meet,
It jokes, "I'm tall but can't find my feet!"

Surrounded by sand, it still finds a way,
To sip on the sun through the vibrant day.
"Come closer," it shouts, "I'll tell you a lie,
I'm more than a plant, I'm a wiggly guy!"

The cactus crew rolls its eyes in delight,
As the leaning sprout shares its tales of flight.
"Living on laughs and a dream or two,
I plant myself here just to amuse you!"

So here's to the ones who don't fit the mold,
With wit like a fountain, sharp and bold.
In the lean and the laugh, we take a stand,
Creating lush fun on this barren land!

The Flora of Fortress

In a fortress of thorns where the giggles roam,
Plants poke their heads with a heart of foam.
"Not just a defense, we're also a show,
With puns in our spines, we steal the show!"

When prickle meets humor, it sparks a delight,
Creating a garden of laughter and light.
"Need a shield? Oh, I'm happy to lend,
But don't expect it from a prickly friend!"

The flowers burst forth in brilliant hues,
With jokes about rain when a drought ensues.
In this fortress of fun, we thrive with glee,
As blossoms unravel their comic decree!

So here's to the flora that guards with a grin,
Cackling at life as it happens within.
In the landscape of laughter, forever we grow,
With fun in the soil and sunshine on show!

The Dance of the Desert Flora

In the sun, they twist and sway,
With spines that glimmer, oh what a display!
They shimmy to tunes of the desert breeze,
Giggling softly as they aim to please.

A party of flora, wild and free,
Each with a partner, can you see?
The yucca's got moves, the agave one too,
While prickly pals poke at one or two!

With laughter and color in sandy scenes,
These plants throw a bash with their leafy routines.
When the sun sets low, they gather near,
Swapping tall tales with a cactus cheer!

So join the fun, don't miss the chance,
To dance with the desert in a spiny romance!
A two-step among the succulents so fine,
In this wacky fiesta of bumpy design.

The Soul of Succulence

In the heart of the desert, a laugh arises,
From fleshy friends telling witty surprises.
With quirky shapes and colors so bright,
They gossip like neighbors, from morning to night.

A chubby little guy with a roguish grin,
Says to a tall one, "You think you can win?"
"Look at my curves and my juicy delight,
I'm the snack of the season, just take a bite!"

Spines on the outside, but sweet on the in,
Together they chuckle, let the games begin!
They tell of the rain that once graced their heads,
And the days they spent counting the stars in their beds.

With friends like these in the sun-soaked land,
Life is a hoot, it's perfectly grand!
So open your heart to the succulent cheer,
And join in the fun, there's nothing to fear!

Blossom Against the Odds

Out in the cracks of the stony ground,
Flora fight fiercely, refusing to drown.
Tiny blooms pop with a jubilant cheer,
Defying the odds, they will persevere.

With petals so bright, they burst into song,
While the world around them seems gray and wrong.
With grit and grace, they laugh at despair,
Each little flower is a dare to compare!

They wink at the sun, and dance with the moon,
Singing to shadows, on wild afternoons.
Every burst of color is a joke on the fate,
These rebels of nature, they really create!

So heed their message, and join in the fun,
Embrace every challenge until the day's done.
For where there's a will, and a will to bloom,
Life's just a comedy, and they'll clear the gloom!

Resilience in the Rock

Cracks in the pavement, that's where they hide,
Little green warriors with nowhere to bide.
They laugh at the storms and the toughest of winds,
For every tough story, a funny tale spins.

"Knock knock!" says one, peeking out with a grin,
"Who's there?" asks another, just giddy within.
"Orange juice!" they chime, "Orange you glad?"
In the face of tough times, they refuse to be sad!

Resilient champions of dry, sun-baked days,
With humor that brightens the harshest of rays.
They twist and they turn, with a spirit so bold,
These rock-solid jokers turn iron to gold!

So tip your hat to the ones that survive,
Each quip a reminder that they're very alive.
In the face of the rocky, the prickly, the grime,
They keep the fun rolling, one leaf at a time!

The Green Guardians

In the desert, spiky and bright,
Stand the guardians, a peculiar sight.
With their arms stretched wide,
They wave at the sun with pride.

When the wind whispers a playful tease,
They dance a jig, if you please!
Sharp little fellows in a row,
Who knew they had this much show?

Water drops are scarce, that's a fact,
Yet they wear their dryness like a pact.
Stealing the scene with no regret,
These green guys, you just can't forget.

With a grin as wide as the desert's span,
They make every sunbaked moment a jam.
Who needs a drink when you have this fun?
In the parched land, they're number one!

Life in the Parched Expanse

In the heat of day, they stand so proud,
Wearing hats of dust, like a quirky crowd.
Their roots dig deep, but their humor's high,
Making the sun most watchful cry.

They share tall tales of the last big rain,
While neighbors chuckle and groan in vain.
"Oh please, dear friend, more water's a tease,
We're fine right here with a gentle breeze."

With arms outstretched, they greet the night,
Telling the stars jokes that feel just right.
While owls roll their eyes, they laugh and roar,
Adventures await, oh, what's in store?

Who knew the drought would spark such glee?
In this wild land, it's a comedy spree.
With every poke and every grin,
Life's parched expanse is a fun-filled win!

Echoes of the Sun-Baked Soil

In the soil where warmth does sing,
Lies a drama, a prickly fling.
With whispers of seeds that chuckle and tease,
They plot their rise, taking it with ease.

The sun hollers down, "Can't take a break!"
Yet the little green jesters just laugh and shake.
They share sly winks at the gathering breeze,
"Hey, let's hop and sway, like leaves in trees!"

Mirages dance, the desert's own jest,
As each plant competes for the title of best.
Beneath all that spiky and stoic charm,
Lies a funny spirit, causing no harm.

With echoes of laughter in parched, baked ground,
The humor of nature is joyfully found.
Who knew such life could thrive in a drought?
While the sun burns bright, they romp about!

The Thicket of Time

In a thicket where time stands still,
Plants have secrets—they love a thrill.
With age-old jokes passed from thorn to thorn,
They whisper 'round shadows, each prickles worn.

"Hey, why didn't the flower get a date?"
"Too much thistle, just couldn't wait!"
The puns are sharp, like their spiky guise,
Every chuckle holds a wise surprise.

As the sun drips low, golden and bright,
Even the rocks join in the delight.
The tale of the ages, a saga untold,
Turns every frown into laughter bold.

In this timeless lush sprawl of green,
Where laughter and light become a routine.
Here's to the spines with a comic twist,
In the thicket of time, joy can't be missed!

A Parable of Prickles

In desert lands where sun does shine,
Stood a prickly fellow, quite divine.
He'd wave his arms, a spiky dance,
While passing lizards took a chance.

With jagged hugs that left them sore,
They laughed and rolled upon the floor.
The wisdom there, if you may glean,
Beware the hugs that prick and glean.

A lesson learned in sunny rays,
To choose your friends in quirky ways.
For laughter blooms in thorny times,
When prickle-pals share silly rhymes.

So next you see a plant so bold,
Remember tales that humor told.
With twinkling spines and laughter loud,
The prickly ones can join the crowd.

The Clandestine Green

In a corner of the dusty ground,
A secret plant was nearly found.
With sneaky spikes and crafty glee,
It hid away from all to see.

"Oh, I'm just grass!" it said in jest,
While critters puzzled on a quest.
A sandwich maketh not a meal,
Without some prickles to conceal!

The ants had meetings, very sly,
Underneath that sneaky guy.
With whispers shared of food divine,
They plotted parties 'round the spine.

A jolly feast with pricks and puns,
They danced and sang, had loads of fun.
In greenest shades, they made a scene,
A party sprouting from the unseen.

Journey Through the Arid

In a land of dry and sandy hue,
A wanderer with dreams in view.
He packed his hopes in prickly gear,
A comical sight, but oh so dear!

Through golden dunes and blazing sun,
He stumbled on, still full of fun.
His backpack poked with spikes and flair,
Made every tumble feel like air.

"Oh joy!" he shouted, "What a ride!"
As tumbleweeds began to glide.
He laughed aloud at every fall,
For in the end, he'd rise through all!

With every step, he found delight,
A prickly path became so bright.
And when he reached the oasis grand,
He raised his arms, the desert's stand.

Tenacity in Texture

Oh, what a plant, so bold and bright,
With armor tough but hearts so light.
They'll say, "Aren't you scary, too?"
While sharing laughs and morning dew.

Each little spike a story tells,
Of growing up where sunshine dwells.
With every poke, a chuckle grows,
In sandy lands where friendship flows.

So when you see them on your way,
Just give a cheer and shout, "Hooray!"
For life's too short to feel a sting,
Let humor reign and laughter spring!

In textures tough, we find our cheer,
With prickly pals, there's naught to fear.
Embrace the funny, hug the strange,
In every oddness, life will change.

Resilient Beauty in Spines

In a garden full of thorns, she prances,
Wearing armor, turning glances.
With a wink and a sway, quite the sight,
Making the desert dance with delight.

She laughs at the sun, so bold and bright,
Living life like a silly little sprite.
Her spines a shield, her spirit a tease,
In the driest places, she finds the breeze.

A Dance with the Drought

When the rain forgets to drop,
She throws a wild party, not a flop.
With twirls of dust and sandy shows,
She makes the ground break out in prose.

Gather 'round, all you thirsty folks,
Watch the little bloom play her jokes.
She'll tell you tales of what was wet,
While sipping sunshine, with no regret.

Legends of the Drylands

In the land where the sun is king,
Lives a succulent, doing her bling.
With stories tall and a grin so wide,
She'll spin yarns of the great dry ride.

Oh, the hares all wish they could stay,
To hear her tales of a hot, hot day.
While the tumbleweeds tumble and talk,
She just chuckles; it's her sidewalk.

Windswept Blooms

With a shake and a shimmy, she greets the breeze,
Waving her arms like she's lost in ease.
Spinning around with a laugh and a spin,
Who thought a plant could look this akin?

The wind whispers secrets behind her back,
As she puffs up proudly, never lacks.
In a land where the heat never fades,
Her quirky charm is how she parades.

Portraits of a Thorny Life

In the desert sun, I take my stand,
With prickly arms and dreams so grand.
I wave to the sun, not a care in sight,
But to hug me tight? That's just not right!

My friends are the lizards, green and wise,
They giggle and scurry; oh, what a prize!
They tell me tales of the foolish folk,
Who think they can sit without a poke.

A bloom up top, so bright and bold,
But beneath it all, I'm not so gold.
Soft and squishy? Not quite my style,
But if you're up for fun, stay for a while!

In the land where nothing grows too tall,
I stand as a king, though short in the hall.
Life's prickly lessons, oh what joy!
Embrace the silly—desert's my toy!

Arid Secrets and Sunlit Highs

Under the blue skies, I take my stance,
With secrets so dry, not a bit of romance.
Every tumbleweed tells a joke or two,
As I shimmy and sway like I'm part of the crew.

The sun is a prankster, so bold and bright,
It laughs at my spines, oh what a sight!
I chuckle along, with my needle-like glee,
And sip on the sunshine like it's sweet tea.

When rain clouds do gather, the buzz is alive,
All the cactus folks start to jive and thrive.
But the moment it passes, we all just sigh,
"Looks like we're stuck in our sunbaked pie!"

With a dance in my roots, I revel in play,
For life in the heat is a comical sway.
With shadows as friends, I take a long rest,
In this sunlit land, I feel truly blessed!

Journeys of the Desert Dwellers

Oh, the journeys we make under the blazing sun,
With prickles and laughter, oh, what fun!
We wander and ponder in sandy delight,
Sharing wild stories under the moonlight.

A tumbleweed rolls; it's a merry dance,
While I stand my ground, not giving a chance.
The saguaros gossip, their arms in the air,
Measuring how tall they can grow without care!

In the mirage ahead, a fountain appears,
But it's just a cool prank, oh the roars and the cheers!
We fall to the sand, oh what a surprise,
Life never gets old with these funny guys.

When the night sets in, we share our tales,
Of daring escapades and gusty gales.
In the desert's embrace, we laugh until dawn,
For the joy of our journeys will always live on!

The Language of Aridity

In a land where the sun dons the silliest hat,
We speak in a tongue known only to that.
A giggle, a poke, in the dry desert air,
The voices of cactus will always declare!

With prickly diplomacy, I wave at a tree,
A brother in arms, as green as can be.
"Let's share our secrets," I say with a grin,
As he shrugs and replies, "Where would we begin?"

The wind carries laughter like a soft serenade,
While the shadows of dusk make a grand masquerade.
We dance on the dunes, it's a fabulous scene,
With the language of aridity, life's just more keen!

So raise up a toast with the sun's golden rays,
To the silly and prickly, we'll sing out our praise.
In this warm-hearted desert, we'll never grow old,
For our tales are as rich as the legends retold!

Seasons of the Succulent

In spring, they dance under the sun,
Wearing hats made of dust, oh what fun!
They giggle and sway with a prickly grace,
While bees take selfies, it's quite the space.

Summer rolls in, it's a sizzle show,
Succulents sipping water, moving slow.
They swap stories of storms and rain,
While lizards join in, quite uncontained.

Autumn arrives with a colorful twist,
A party of colors, none can resist.
The leaves twist in laughter, stories unfold,
As the sun dips low, turning hearts bold.

Winter whispers, but they're still so bright,
With jackets of frost, they shimmer at night.
A comical sight, they all huddle tight,
Sharing sweet tales under starlit light.

Echoes in the Canyons

In canyons deep, the laughter roars,
Echoing tales of plant galores.
With arms all spiky, they tease the breeze,
Swaying and shaking, just like the trees.

A tumbleweed bounces, trying to play,
While shadows dance, leading astray.
The rocks start chuckling, they can't hold it in,
As the sun sets low, let the fun begin!

Rattlesnakes giggle, wearing silly hats,
While saguaros strike poses in chat.
They boast of their height, proud and so tall,
While shadows below just laugh at it all.

Stars wink above, joining the scene,
As night falls down, a whimsical dream.
In the canyon's embrace, where the echoes play,
The plants tell secrets in the funniest way.

Desert Whispers

In the desert sun, whispers abound,
Funny tales of the wiry and round.
Sandy children with giggles galore,
Trading cactus tales, who could ask for more?

A lizard on a rock strikes a pose so grand,
While the prickly plants offer a hand.
They share all the gossip, a succulent choir,
Under the heat waves, they never get tired.

A playful breeze stirs the desert air,
Carrying chuckles from far everywhere.
The tumbleweeds tumble, they roll and they dance,
Creating a scene that's pure happenstance.

At twilight's door, the stories unfold,
Laughter and whispers in colors bold.
Desert life's wacky, with hearty delight,
Where every heart feels the joy of the night.

Spines of Silence

In a patch of silence, spines stand tall,
Each one has a secret, each a tale small.
With a nudge and a wink, they look to the skies,
In their prickly silence, the fun sneaks by.

One spine starts giggling, it can't keep contained,
While others join in, so unrestrained.
The sun rolls by, casting smiles so wide,
In the quietest moments, joy can't abide.

Peek at the shadows, what do you see?
A parade of plants, quite the jubilee!
With every sunbeam, their laughter ignites,
A spiny ensemble under starry nights.

When silence meets laughter, the spines intertwine,
Creating a symphony, oh, it's sublime!
So here in the quiet, let joy not be still,
For laughter and silence, they dance with a thrill.

Dances with Drought

In the desert, I take a twirl,
My partner's prickles make me whirl.
The sun's a spotlight, hot and bright,
We dance till shadows fade from sight.

A tumbleweed joins in my spree,
We laugh at how parched we can be.
The breeze suggests a waltz, quite bold,
But it's mostly just a dust bowl hold.

My water bottle's half a tease,
With sips of air, I sway with ease.
The lizards clap their tiny hands,
While I elevate my sandy plans.

A joshua tree joins in the groove,
With limbs that twist and brightly move.
In this sun-soaked, silly affair,
Drought turns laughter into thin air.

Grit and Grits

In the skillet, grit's a dish,
Baked in sun, who knew I'd wish?
Each grain a nugget, rough yet sweet,
Together, they form a spicy treat.

A roadrunner zips past my plate,
Singing songs of the desert fate.
I sprinkle laughter on my meal,
'Cause every bite is a funny deal.

With thorns like forks, we dig right in,
Each chew a giggle, wild and thin.
A tumble of flavors caught in jest,
Grit and grits, they pass the test.

When life's too tough, just add some spice,
A pinch of humor will suffice.
In this desert dining, we proclaim,
Grit and grits—the wildest game!

The Language of Thorns

Communing softly with the air,
My prickly friends have tales to share.
They talk in whispers, sharp and clear,
Each thorn a story, each laugh a cheer.

The lizards listen with big, wide eyes,
As spiky genres make us laugh and cry.
A sonnet told by a pointy friend,
Ends with a poke, but humor won't bend.

Banding together, we jest and jibe,
In a world that's dry, we dance, we vibe.
With every poke, a punchline blooms,
Thorns are the poets in the dusty rooms.

So let's raise a glass to thorns so bright,
In a language full of silly delight.
Every jab and prick is worth the pain,
As laughter echoes in the desert plain!

Heat Over Reflection

The sun blares down, a fiery boss,
Mirrors shimmer, reflecting gloss.
I wave to the heat with a goofy grin,
It waves back, saying, 'You're in!'

Sweat is my makeup, dripping style,
I take my stroll, dance just a while.
With every bounce, I shake the sand,
The sun applauds, can you understand?

My thoughts get hazy, like the mirage,
Is that a cactus? Or just a barrage?
But I laugh as I trudge through the scene,
Heat makes the world look rather keen.

So here I toast to the blazing sphere,
With a wink for laughter, that's so dear.
The heat's a friend, so let's reflect,
In this hot mess, we can connect!

Oasis in a Thistle Wind

In the desert's dance, winds twist and twirl,
Sandstorms tease, giving prickly curls.
A mirage sways with cheeky grace,
While lizards laugh, a sunbaked race.

A drink of water? Just a hoot!
The barrel's dry, not a single root.
A party planned, yet no one shows,
Just me and the dust, in my thorny clothes.

The tumbleweeds roll, a sight so grand,
They dance like fools, all unplanned.
A heatwave's joke, a trickster's plan,
I sip thin air, the desert's fan.

But oh, the night, when stars alight,
The cooler breeze, a sweet delight.
I toast to friends made of spines and shade,
In this laughable place, where pranks are laid.

The Silent Sentinel

A prickly guard stands tall and proud,
Quietly chuckling, never too loud.
With arms spread wide, he blocks the sun,
Who's he scaring? No one thinks he's fun.

His buddies tease him, 'You're way too tough!'
But in reality, he's just a little gruff.
Each visitor fears they might get poked,
While he stands still, laughing and choked.

The birds find him quite a perfect mate,
They perch on his spikes, it's first-rate.
He's a party host for the feathered crowd,
Who chirp and sing, lively and loud.

In this wild expanse where heat waves soar,
Our sentinel guards, forever more.
So here's to the one who stands with flair,
A silent joker with a prickly hair.

Blooms Amidst the Barren

In a world so dry, blooms pop up bright,
Dancing among thorns, a quirky sight.
They giggle and sway in the searing sun,
Wildflowers laughing, just having fun.

A flower's dream? To live in style,
With colors that dazzle and make you smile.
But hey, what's this? A prickly foe!
They trade playful jabs in the warm-flow glow.

A bumblebee buzzes, looking quite lost,
He hurries through thistles, oh what a cost!
Yet blooms keep laughing, swaying their heads,
"Join us, dear bee! No need for treads!"

In barren earth, they paint the scene,
A riot of colors, lively and keen.
So here's to blooms that defy the fates,
In the laughing land where the arid waits.

Thorns and Dreams

Dreams grow tall in a prickly place,
Where thorns can hug, with a spiky embrace.
A jester's cap is worn with flair,
In the wild green patch, filled with care.

Each thorn has a tale, oh what a ride,
They poke and they prod, but still abide.
A wish upon a spire, pointy and neat,
With laughter echoing—what a treat!

Underneath the stars, the stories unfold,
Of spiky romance that's brave and bold.
They twirl and they leap, these whimsical dreams,
In the heart of the desert, laughter beams.

So when you wander where thorns do reign,
Remember the joy that hides in the pain.
For in every prick, there's laughter, it seems,
Thorns and dreams, the best of schemes.

Desert Whispers

In the land where the sand dunes sway,
A prickly plant dreams of the day,
To have a sip of a cool, sweet drink,
But all it gets is a wink and a blink.

The sun's so bright, it wears a hat,
While lizards dance, quick as a cat,
A cactus tried to bust a move,
But its spines went wild, oh what a groove!

A tumbleweed rolled by with style,
The cactus chuckled, "Stay a while!"
But tumbleweed just gave a twirl,
And off it went to spin and whirl.

Under the stars, the critters cheer,
As the moon whispers, "Don't you fear,"
In this humorous plant life spree,
Nature's laughter is wild and free.

Spines of Solitude

A lone green spire stands all alone,
Surrounded by muck that nobody's grown,
It throws a party for one or two,
But only misses the cheatgrass crew.

It sent invitations all around,
But nobody came, just silence found,
So it danced with shadows under the sun,
Bouncing to rhythms, oh what fun!

A curious rabbit hopped by in glee,
And asked, "What's cooking? Can I join thee?"
The cactus laughed, "Just bring your ears,
And perhaps some punch, to toast to my fears."

In moments of solitude, funny and bright,
Even a prickly boy can take flight,
For in this vast land, laughter prevails,
With spines of solitude, tell glorious tales.

Dunes of Resilience

In a sea of sand, so vast and far,
A cactus stood with dreams like a star,
To brave the storm and dance in rain,
Though mostly it squabbled, "Oh, what a pain!"

It watched a lizard take a graceful leap,
While it just stood, stuck in an eternal creep,
"Move with the wind," the sands would sing,
While it just chuckled, pretending to swing.

The clouds rolled in, a joke on its side,
The cactus braced, puffing up with pride,
But a tiny drizzle made it giggle,
"Is that all you've got? Now that's a riddle!"

Through troubles and trials, it wouldn't back down,
In dunes of resilience, wore laughter as crown,
With wind in its spines, it wobbled with might,
An odd little hero, in the wide desert light.

Prickly Tales Under the Sun

Beneath the warmth of a blazing sun,
A prickly fellow thinks life is fun,
He tells old tales to the geared-up ants,
Who giggle and wiggle in their dance-pants.

"Once I tripped on a rock in the night,
And swore I'd never take that flight,
But here I am, still living wide,
With spines for protection, what a ride!"

The gophers pause, ears perk in joy,
"Tell us more, oh spiny boy!"
With every tale, the humor grows,
As less serious cactus life just glows.

Under the sun, friendships bloom,
In prickly patches where laughter zooms,
And every spine's a reminder to jest,
That life in the desert can surely be blessed.

A Garden of Thorns

In the garden where spiky things play,
Plants wear armor, come what may.
Laughing at bugs that dare to intrude,
In their prickly realm, they're quite rude.

Sunbathers bask in the blazing sun,
With arms wide open, they shout, "What fun!"
A dance with the breeze, but a sting is near,
Watch your step, my friend—there's danger here!

Rooted in dirt, but dreams touch the sky,
Yet, their sharpness makes neighbors sigh.
They wave to the toads, they wink at the sun,
In this world of thorns, life's never undone.

With a flourish of green, they thrive, no doubt,
In their prickly paradise, they'll never pout.
A prick on the finger, a laugh shared in jest,
Amidst all the thorns, they still feel blessed.

The Stillness Within

In silence they stand, looking all cool,
While secretly thinking they're the top jewel.
With spines all around, they keep things light,
Who knew they'd be the butt of a spike-filled fright?

Their patience tested when summer is hot,
Gossiping whispers, 'Hey, give it a shot!'
A stillness that hints at the mischief below,
Like they're planning a comedy show.

Blossoms like fireworks atop their heads,
They throw wild parties when nobody's fed.
"Oh bother," they say, "we're tough, that's the trick!"
But deep down inside, they tug at the stick.

In solitude's embrace, they'll crack a grin,
Prickly outside but fluffy within.
Their stillness is laughter, a joke to behold,
In a world where the boldest are often quite old.

Serenity Among Spines

Amidst all the dangers, they sit with glee,
Observing the world from their prickly tree.
"We've got it figured out," they proudly declare,
While poking the gentle who dare to come near.

A serene parade in a spiky prime,
They wave to the flowers, "We're doing just fine!"
Each hostile point is just part of the plan,
For the amusement of creatures—oh, what a jam!

In shorts and T-shirts, they revel in charm,
Hot days are perfect, no fear of alarm.
Spinning tales in the breeze, their laughter a gift,
Among spines and thorns, they dance and they drift.

With gossip and giggles, they throw a grand fête,
Where everyone's welcome—as long as they're straight.
In perfect formation, they humor the night,
With serenity found in their own prickly plight.

Blooming Under Pressure

Under pressure, they flaunt their great style,
Spines all a-glimmer, each one with a smile.
They jest about life with a wink and a nudge,
"Don't fear our arms; they're just a small grudge!"

Flower crowns glowing, they strut with delight,
"Life's a competition, let's all take flight!"
When the sun bears down, and the moisture is sparse,
The party erupts, oh, how they can arse!

"With blossoms that pop and colors galore,
Under pressure, we shake and explore!"
Showcasing flair, while the others just wilt,
They thrive on adversity, built up with grit.

So here's to the blooms that laugh at the heat,
They chuckle and giggle while all take a seat.
In a world full of thorns, let's raise a cheer,
For the ones who bloom, with hearts full of cheer!

www.ingramcontent.com/pod-product-compliance
Lightning Source LLC
Chambersburg PA
CBHW072141200426
43209CB00051B/228